ANACONDA VS. JAGUAR

BY THOMAS K. ADAMSON

TORQUE™

BELLWETHER MEDIA · MINNEAPOLIS, MN

Torque brims with excitement
perfect for thrill-seekers of all kinds.
Discover daring survival skills, explore
uncharted worlds, and marvel at mighty
engines and extreme sports. In *Torque* books,
anything can happen. Are you ready?

This edition first published in 2020 by Bellwether Media, Inc.

No part of this publication may be reproduced in whole or in part without
written permission of the publisher.
For information regarding permission, write to Bellwether Media, Inc.,
Attention: Permissions Department,
6012 Blue Circle Drive, Minnetonka, MN 55343.

Library of Congress Cataloging-in-Publication Data

Names: Adamson, Thomas K., 1970- author.
Title: Anaconda vs. Jaguar / by Thomas K. Adamson.
   Other titles: Anaconda versus jaguar
Description: Minneapolis, MN : Bellwether Media, Inc., 2020. | Series:
   Torque: animal battles | Includes bibliographical references and index.
   | Audience: Ages 7-12 | Audience: Grades 3-7 | Summary: "Amazing
   photography accompanies engaging information about anacondas and
   jaguars. The combination of high-interest subject matter and light text
   is intended for students in grades 3 through 7"– Provided by publisher.
Identifiers: LCCN 2019030617 (print) | LCCN 2019030618 (ebook) | ISBN
   9781644871553 (library binding) | ISBN 9781618918352 (ebook)
Subjects: LCSH: Anaconda–Juvenile literature. | Jaguar–Juvenile
   literature.
Classification: LCC QL666.O63 A326 2020 (print) | LCC QL666.O63 (ebook)
   | DDC 597.96/7–dc23
LC record available at https://lccn.loc.gov/2019030617
LC ebook record available at https://lccn.loc.gov/2019030618

Text copyright © 2020 by Bellwether Media, Inc. TORQUE and associated
logos are trademarks and/or registered trademarks of Bellwether Media, Inc.

Editor: Christina Leaf   Designer: Andrea Schneider

Printed in the United States of America, North Mankato, MN.

TABLE OF CONTENTS

THE COMPETITORS

The **rain forest** is home to two fierce fighters.
Jaguars are the biggest cats in the Americas.
They have a bite strong enough to crush bones!

Pound for pound, anacondas are larger than all other snakes. Anacondas are **constrictors**. These **reptiles** squeeze their **prey** before swallowing it whole. But could an anaconda defeat a jaguar?

JAGUAR PROFILE

0   2 FEET   4 FEET   6 FEET   8 FEET

BODY LENGTH
UP TO 6 FEET (1.8 METERS)

HEIGHT
2.6 FEET (0.8 METERS) AT THE SHOULDER

WEIGHT
UP TO 350 POUNDS (160 KILOGRAMS)

HABITAT

RAIN FORESTS

JAGUAR RANGE

☐ RANGE

Black jaguars have spots, too. They are hard to see under the black fur. You would not want to get close enough to see them!

ROSETTES

Jaguars live in the rain forests of South America. These **predators** live and hunt alone. They are known for black spots called **rosettes** on their tan and orange coats. Some jaguars are black.

Jaguars are great swimmers and like to be near water. These **mammals** also hide in the branches of trees.

GREEN ANACONDA

There are four **species** of anaconda. Green anacondas are the heaviest. They live in the swamps and rivers of the Amazon rain forest. They spend a lot of time in the water. The water supports their weight. This helps them move faster in water than on land.

Anacondas have been known to eat jaguars. They also eat birds, turtles, deer, and capybaras.

GREEN ANACONDA PROFILE

12 INCHES

HEIGHT

12 INCHES
(30 CENTIMETERS)
IN DIAMETER

WEIGHT

UP TO 550 POUNDS
(249 KILOGRAMS)

LENGTH

UP TO 33 FEET
(10 METERS)

HABITAT

RAIN FORESTS

GREEN ANACONDA RANGE

■ **RANGE**

SECRET WEAPONS

Anacondas and jaguars both use fearsome bites in attacks. Anacondas are not **venomous**. They use their six rows of teeth to keep prey from getting away.

1,500 POUNDS
PER SQUARE INCH

JAGUAR BITE FORCE

162 POUNDS
PER SQUARE INCH

HUMAN BITE FORCE

For jaguars, it is the powerful bite that kills its prey. They kill with one strong bite on the animal's skull.

POWERFUL JAWS

LARGE TEETH

LARGE CLAWS

Jaguars also use their sharp claws as weapons. The claws dig into prey to hold on tight. Jaguars can **retract** their claws. This keeps the claws protected and sharp.

SECRET WEAPONS

ANACONDA

SPOTS FOR HIDING

STRONG BODY

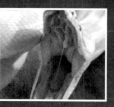
SIX ROWS OF TEETH

Anacondas use their whole body as a weapon!
They wrap themselves around prey. Their squeezing
strength does not allow animals to get away.

ATTACK MOVES

Both anacondas and jaguars are surprisingly good swimmers. Anacondas hide in **murky** water. Their eyes and nose are on top of their heads so they can peek above the water

Jaguars are also great at using water to their **advantage**. They swiftly and silently swim to approach prey.

Both attackers wait and **ambush** their prey. Anacondas attack when prey approaches the water. These snakes move quickly for their size. They latch onto prey with their teeth and coil themselves around it.

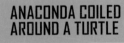

ANACONDA COILED
AROUND A TURTLE

OPEN WIDE

Anaconda jaws stretch to open extra wide.

The name jaguar means "he who kills with one leap."

Jaguars' rosettes hide them from prey. When prey gets close, the cats **lunge**. Their speed and **stealth** provide an effective surprise attack.

Unlike other big cats, jaguars finish off prey with a skull bite. The jaguar then drags it off to a safe place to eat.

Anacondas pull prey into the water as they squeeze to finish the attack. This move also helps the snakes get large animals into position for swallowing.

SQUEEZE FORCE

ANACONDA SQUEEZE STRENGTH
(90 POUNDS PER SQUARE INCH)

=

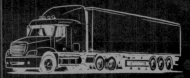

HAVING A SEMI TRUCK PARKED ON YOU!

READY, FIGHT!

A jaguar peers into the water, looking for a quick snack. An anaconda's eyes peek just above the surface. Splash! The anaconda lunges. It wraps around the cat.

The jaguar claws the snake but cannot escape. The anaconda drags the jaguar into the water and stretches its mouth wide. This bold anaconda took on a fierce hunter. But its strength was too much for the jaguar!

SQUEEZE PLAY

The anaconda's squeezing prevents
prey's blood from flowing properly.
The animal's organs and brain shut down.
Soon, the prey's heart stops beating.

GLOSSARY

advantage—something an animal has or can do better than their enemy

ambush—to carry out a surprise attack

constrictors—snakes that use their bodies to squeeze prey until it dies

lunge—to move forward quickly

mammals—warm-blooded animals that have backbones and feed their young milk

murky—muddy and unclear

predators—animals that hunt other animals for food

prey—animals that are hunted by other animals for food

rain forest—a thick, green forest that receives a lot of rain

reptiles—cold-blooded animals that have backbones and lay eggs

retract—to pull back in

rosettes—the black spots on a jaguar

species—kinds of animals

stealth—the state of being secretive or unnoticed

venomous—able to produce venom; venom is a kind of poison made by some snakes.

TO LEARN MORE

AT THE LIBRARY

Gregory, Josh. *Anacondas*. New York, N.Y.: Children's Press, 2016.

Krieger, Emily. *Animal Smackdown: Surprising Animal Matchups with Surprising Results*. Washington D.C.: National Geographic Kids, 2018.

Vink, Amanda. *Jaguars*. New York, N.Y.: PowerKids Press, 2020.

ON THE WEB

FACTSURFER

Factsurfer.com gives you a safe, fun way to find more information.

1. Go to www.factsurfer.com

2. Enter "anaconda vs. jaguar" into the search box and click $\mathcal{Q}$.

3. Select your book cover to see a list of related web sites.

INDEX

ambush, 16
attacks, 10, 16, 17, 19
bite, 4, 10, 11, 18
cats, 4, 17, 18, 20
claws, 12, 20
coil, 16
color, 7
constrictors, 5
eyes, 14, 20
habitat, 4, 6, 7, 8, 9
hide, 7, 17
hunt, 7, 20
jaws, 16
lunge, 17, 20
mammals, 7
nose, 14
predators, 7
prey, 5, 8, 10, 11, 12, 15, 16, 17, 18, 19
rain forest, 4, 6, 7, 8, 9

range, 4, 6, 7, 8, 9
reptiles, 5
retract, 12
rosettes, 7, 17
size, 5, 6, 9, 16
snakes, 5, 16, 19, 20
species, 8
speed, 8, 16, 17
spots, 7, 8
squeeze, 5, 13, 19, 21
strength, 13, 20
swallowing, 5, 19
swim, 7, 14, 15
teeth, 10, 16
venomous, 10
water, 7, 8, 14, 15, 16, 19, 20
weapons, 12, 13